Original title:
The House of Echoing Souls

Copyright © 2025 Creative Arts Management OÜ
All rights reserved.

Author: Alec Davenport
ISBN HARDBACK: 978-1-80587-213-9
ISBN PAPERBACK: 978-1-80587-683-0

Lanterns of Lost Time

In corners where shadows like gossip grow,
Old lanterns flicker with tales they know.
A cat in a top hat, a dance on the rug,
Whispers of secrets make time feel a shrug.

Tickling the floors with their giggles and squeaks,
Dust bunnies hoot in their silly critiques.
A worried old lamp post with glasses too thick,
Claims it once dated a rather bold brick.

Veils of Dusty Remembrance

Veils of dust waltz on forgotten old chairs,
Where uninvited memories linger and stare.
Button-eyed dolls plot a mischievous scheme,
While clocks play hopscotch in a whimsical dream.

Lace curtains giggle at a ghost on the floor,
Who's too shy to dance but just can't ignore.
A parrot in plaid insists on the news,
Extra, extra! Read about the old blues!

Ghost Notes of Abandoned Rooms

In rooms where echoes play hopscotch and hide,
Ghost notes frolic together, side by side.
A piano that's flat sings in perfect repose,
While a ghostly old chef bakes invisible dough.

Pictures above are quite the feisty lot,
Debating on who got their whiskers caught.
A chandelier yawns, its crystals all cling,
To the rambunctious tunes of the spirits that sing.

The Abode of Lamenting Hearts

Hearts in this dwelling wear shoes made of rubber,
They bounce and they squeak, oh my, what a hubbub!
Knocking on walls, they sing off-key tunes,
While chairs throw themselves into optimistic swoons.

A wishbone whispers, 'Let's party tonight!'
As cornbread takes flight, what a curious sight!
With every wrong turn, laughter echoes so bright,
Even the shadows all join in the light!

Voices Carried on the Wind

Whispers swirl in breezy jest,
Laughter carried, never at rest.
Hats and shoes in a playful chase,
Echoes of giggles fill the space.

Doors creak like a wise old sage,
Poking fun at the passing age.
Curtains dance with a cheeky grin,
As shadows poke their heads right in.

Tapestries of Untold Stories

Threads of laughter, woven tight,
Dancing patterns in morning light.
Each knot's a tale that's ready to show,
Where socks and slippers often go.

A silver spoon with a sassy flair,
Turns to gossip with no care.
Behind the walls, the secrets sigh,
While spoons roll their eyes and comply.

The Ghostlight's Embrace

In the dead of night, lights flicker bright,
Chasing shadows, what a sight!
A ghostly figure trips on the rug,
With laughter echoing like a snug bug.

Lamps complain of their nightly toil,
While giggles rise from the dusty soil.
In the corner, a clock's funny chime,
Counts the giggles, one at a time.

Shadows Weaving Through the Rooms

A shadow hops and skips in glee,
Telling tales of mystery.
It pulls a chair, inviting a seat,
Where the echoes and laughter all meet.

Under the table, a game unfolds,
With jolly whispers and daring bolds.
Every nook seems to join the fun,
In this playful air, they all run.

Comfort of a Fading Echo

In rooms where whispers play,
Laughter bounces, then drifts away.
A chair groans with every joke,
While shadows dance and mirrors poke.

A ghost drops a spoon with a clink,
What's that noise? It's hard to think.
The cat's eyes roll with delight,
As echoes giggle through the night.

When Walls Speak in Sighs

These walls have stories to tell,
Of secrets and laughter, all is well.
They sigh and creak with delight,
As the clock ticks close to midnight.

A door swings wide with a burst,
Each squeak is a pun, rehearsed.
Oh, the dances that they keep,
In shadows, mischief runs deep.

Vows Sworn in Ghostly Light

At dusk, the candles flicker bright,
Promising laughter, not a fright.
Two joined hands in a wobbly grip,
Swearing vows through a playful quip.

The chandelier sways, it knows the score,
A playful ghost reads from folklore.
With giggles that reverberate,
They seal their love with a wobble rate.

Haunting Melodies of the Night

Tunes play softly on a breeze,
As curtains shimmy with such ease.
The ghostly band doesn't fret,
Just strums and taps on keys, you bet!

With every note, a chuckle flies,
As poltergeists join in surprise.
Their rhythm haunts the sleepy lane,
A raucous sound, not one of pain.

Paeans of the Past On The Wind

In a place where whispers play,
Giggles chase the ghosts away.
Laughter bounces off the wall,
Echoing secrets large and small.

Floors creak with an ancient glee,
Shadows dance, both wild and free.
Portraits grin with mischief bright,
Winking at the startled night.

Brooms take flight, a clumsy crew,
Sweeping up the memories, too.
Jars of jam left to conspire,
Sparkling tales that never tire.

In each corner, old friends jest,
Tickling time with every guest.
Chairs will sway to the refrain,
Where past and present meet again.

Intangible Threads of Home

In a realm where time can't tease,
Spinning yarns in playful breeze.
Threads of laughter weave a quilt,
With every stitch, a story built.

Windows whisper tales of yore,
Doorknobs jingle, 'Come explore!'
The cat plays host, a furry sage,
As we turn the eternal page.

Nightlights hum a silly tune,
While mismatched socks hold court till noon.
Every corner holds a jest,
In this space, we find our rest.

Memories bounce like rubber balls,
Echoing through these sunny halls.
A tapestry of quirky sights,
Here, the mundane turns to flights.

Reflections of Lost Voices

In the attic, shadows play,
Whispers giggle, dance away.
A silver spoon just laughed aloud,
Caught in chatter, feeling proud.

Ghostly gags in every room,
A laughing chair dispels the gloom.
Clattering cups in joyful jest,
They're the jesters—who's the guest?

Beyond the Doorway

Knocking softly, 'Who's in there?'
A sock puppet claims it's unfair.
The door creaks wide, a grin so wide,
A pizza slice danced with pride.

Hats and shoes, they waltz around,
Twirling in the merry sound.
I stepped inside, my heart a-flutter,
A rubber chicken in the clutter.

Faint Footsteps in the Dark

Tip-toeing through the midnight air,
I swear I heard a rubber bear.
He said, "Boo!" with a tickle and wink,
I couldn't help but stop and think.

In the shadows, laughter hides,
A chorus of socks on fun-filled rides.
What a riot, what a glee,
As messy ghosts play tag with me!

The Memory Keeper's Chamber

In a corner, secrets breathe,
A dancing broom with tales to weave.
Each old relic shares a jest,
Forget the past, don't dare to rest!

Pictures wink and mugs will cheer,
With every glance, a chuckle near.
Memory keeper, hold the phone—
Let's laugh about the stuff we've grown!

Whispers in the Hollow Walls

In corners, voices play a tune,
A croaky song from a dusty moon.
"Who dropped the soap?" echoes through,
The laughter in shadows, a silly crew.

Paint peels like giggles, soft and sly,
As whispers flutter, saying goodbye.
"I swear I saw a cat dressed in lace!"
Chasing a phantom, a comical chase.

On wooden beams, a dance of wits,
With silly tales and pun-filled bits.
The clock chimes jokes of days gone by,
As shadows snicker and spirits sigh.

Shadows of Forgotten Lullabies

In the night, shadows sing low,
Lullabies twisted, stealing the show.
"Sleep tight, my dear," a ghostly crow,
Tickles your ears, makes giggles flow.

The faintest hum of a long-lost tune,
Makes even the midnight stars swoon.
"Who needs a blanket?" the shadows coo,
When they can wrap you in laughter too!

Echoes of memories bounce off the walls,
Telling tales of great kitchen brawls.
With wearing grins, they prance and pout,
Lobster in a pot? Now that's what it's about!

Murmurs Beneath the Floorboards

Beneath the floor, where secrets creep,
Whispers concoct plans for a laugh to keep.
"Who is that tapping?" someone will ask,
It's just the floorboards, wearing a mask!

They giggle and jiggle like kids on a spree,
With jokes about socks and tea for three.
"How do you escape a wardrobe's squeeze?"
As echoes erupt in ticklish wheezes.

Each creak is a jest, each rattle a pun,
In the hidden nooks, the fun has begun.
Whispers await in the dust and gloom,
For a comedy hour in the egg-shell room!

Echoes of a Silent Past

Past moments bounce with a curious flair,
Echoes of laughter, a ghostly affair.
"Did you hear that?" a rumble will say,
As spirits come out to join in the play.

In vintage halls, the charm clings tight,
Old-timey jokes make spirits take flight.
"Why did the ghost cross the road?" they ask,
To join the chuckles in a comical mask!

The past is a parade, a quirky delight,
With stories that shimmer in flickering light.
So join in the jests, don't let them fade,
In this rollicking abode, let laughter invade!

Spectral Whispers of Yesterday

In a hall where shadows dwell,
Spooky tales they love to tell.
Yet every creak just makes me laugh,
As ghosts compete for photo graph.

Dusty shoes that dance alone,
They jive back to their own old tone.
With rattling chains, they trip and fall,
A spectral dance-off—what a ball!

Cobwebbed corners hold the jest,
Witty banter from the unrest.
Muffled giggles float in air,
Even phantoms have time to spare.

In these halls of ages past,
The humor here is always vast.
So join the fun, don't be a stranger,
It's a ghostly bash, minus the danger!

Dreams Caught in Twilight's Grasp

When the sun dips low in the sky,
Dreams take a stroll, oh my, oh my!
They trip on clouds, dance on stars,
Chasing fireflies, giggling from afar.

Shadows spin in colors bright,
Bumping into walls, what a sight!
They whisper jokes from times long gone,
As night unfolds and keeps them drawn.

Silliness in dusk's embrace,
Each echo leaves a playful trace.
In this twilight nonsense fest,
Even the moon just can't rest.

Wake me not, I'd rather dream,
Of waltzing shadows, a funny theme.
When dawn approaches with its light,
We'll laugh again, then say goodnight!

Forgotten Corners of the Heart

In a nook where laughter's sound,
Sits a heart that's lost, but found.
With silly secrets tucked away,
In crannies where the shadows play.

Dusty memories start to grin,
As old tunes play, let the fun begin!
The couch sings songs of long-lost friends,
And every reverberation bends.

Under pillows, jokes reside,
A treasure trove of silly pride.
In our hearts, let laughter dwell,
Like whispers one remembers well.

Each echo brings a smiling tear,
Unused corners filled with cheer.
Tripping through this joyous space,
I'll hide my heart to join the chase!

The Silence Between the Echoes

In silence thick, where echoes pause,
The humorous whispers give applause.
A ghostly grin begins to spread,
As chuckles dance around our heads.

Between the sounds of yesteryear,
Laughter echoes, crystal clear.
Like poltergeists in playful mood,
They share their jests without a brood.

Tickled funny, the walls conspire,
To bring us joy, to lift us higher.
As echoes fade, the giggles grow,
In the space where whispers flow.

So hush your heart, and lend an ear,
For laughter's ghost is always near.
In every pause, the fun begins,
As we join in with ghostly grins!

Resonate with Forgotten Laughter

In corners lurk the giggles lost,
Echoes dance, never counting cost.
A chair that creaks like laughter's sigh,
Whispers joke as they drift by.

The clock ticks loud, a goofy tease,
Silly shadows sway with ease.
Old books chuckle, dust bunnies leap,
In every nook, the spirits peep.

Cracks in the wall share a secret grin,
Underneath the rug, some chaos spins.
The chandelier winks, flickers bright,
As ghosts join in for a merry night.

From attic tales to a cellar song,
Laughter rings where souls belong.
Come join the fun, don't miss the cue,
In this realm where joy shines through.

Dust Motions in Moonlight

Moonbeams paint the dusty dance,
While phantoms take their second chance.
They twirl and spin with giddy grace,
Creating smiles on every face.

With every shimmer, a chuckle's heard,
A playful joke, a whispered word.
Dust motes waltz like tiny sprites,
Lighting up the spooky nights.

Shadows giggle in the light,
As spirits soar in flight.
Brooms and mops join in the spree,
Cleaning up the mystery.

The moonlight glows, a silver hue,
And shaking floors seem to woo.
Watch as old chairs jiggle and sway,
Welcome to the wacky display!

Secrets within the Walls

Whispers echo with a quirky flair,
Hiding stories that none would dare.
The wallpaper peels with a wink,
Spilling tales before you think.

Nooks and crannies share old laughs,
As dusty frames hold photographs.
Each creak and pop, a playful jest,
In this space, the fun won't rest.

Light fixtures giggle, swaying low,
While ancient recipes steal the show.
Potions bubble in giddy sets,
Creating mishaps, placing bets.

Beneath the floorboards, secrets hide,
With every giggle, they confide.
Listen close, but do beware,
Laughter echoes everywhere!

The Gathering of Wandering Souls

At twilight's call, the gathering starts,
Wandering souls with giggling hearts.
They meet on floors, under moonlit grace,
In a jolly, ghostly embrace.

Whispers blend in a riotous cheer,
Jokes fly 'round, filling the sphere.
Tales of mishaps and silly schemes,
Rippling laughter, woven dreams.

In kitchen corners, they brew delight,
Spilling stories into the night.
From locked doors to window sills,
Laughter weaves through, oh what thrills!

Old chairs circle, a raucous crowd,
With every jest, they sing out loud.
Join the fun, let spirits twine,
In this realm where humor shines.

Patterned Echoes on the Stairs

Each creak and crack is quite a show,
Pants and laughter as spirits flow.
Ghosts trip over their own two feet,
Making merry on the way to meet.

Lively whispers paint the night,
Jokes that send you into flight.
A banter of pasts, a dance so rare,
Boo! They pop in without a care.

With phantom friends we laugh and sway,
In this peculiar cabaret play.
The stairs, they giggle, the walls, they cheer,
As shadows tumble, out comes a sneer.

So grab a ghost and spin around,
In this place where gaffes are found.
Listen close as they misquote,
"It's not the spirits, it's the floorboards that float!"

Murmurings in the Basement

In the cellar, secrets spill,
Sounds of shuffling evoke a thrill.
Bottles rattle with whispered lore,
Radios stuck on a bygone store.

"Who forgot to pay the ghostly rent?"
Sotto voce, an echo's lament.
The chandelier sways to their jest,
Dancing shadows, a humorous quest.

They argue o'er which haunt is best,
Haunting parties never let them rest.
"Your chains jingle, mine just squeak,
Only the heartiest can take a peek!"

So join the laughter in the gloom,
Where the specters spin and the dust does bloom.
In the basement, it's never a bore,
Just mischief, giggles, and a bit of lore.

A Symphony of Longing

Hollow notes drift through the air,
Banshees croon with a dramatic flair.
Symphonies of sighs chase after dreams,
While lost souls plot their nightly schemes.

"Who's taking the lead in this tune?"
A wraith exclaims under the moon.
A cacophony of wishes collide,
Creating a ruckus they cannot abide.

Mixing laughter with eerie refrains,
The concert continues with giggles and gains.
"Hold my ectoplasm, I'm set to dance!"
"Oh dear, will I vanish? Here's my chance!"

In every refrain, a chuckle's behind,
As echoes of essence leave no one blind.
Each note's a mishap, unique and spry,
In their longing, the spirits fly high.

The Chamber of Requiem

In this room where silence reigns,
A spirited gathering shifts the chains.
"Who ordered pizza for us, again?"
Found out too late, it's a ghostly sin!

Underneath the cloak of night,
They bicker and squabble with sheer delight.
"Ethel, you know you can't eat that pie!"
"Who says? I'm a ghost, watch me try!"

Their shadows flicker, they start a spree,
Guests tumble through walls with glee.
"Bring your quirks, and don't mind the mess,
This requiem's a laugh, nonetheless!"

With spirited bursts and spooky flair,
They bond together in the cool night air.
Requiem? No! Just a riotous time,
Giddy with laughter, they're in their prime.

Sighs Beneath the Ceiling

In the corner, dust bunnies lay,
Gathering tales from yesterday.
They giggle at whispers, hidden away,
While the fridge hums a tuneful ballet.

Beneath the stairs, a sock takes flight,
Chasing the beams of pale moonlight.
A cat plans a heist, an amusing sight,
As chairs slide back in the ghostly night.

Old portraits give winks with a grin,
As echoes of laughter begin to spin.
The clock on the wall rolls its eyes, thin,
While spoons start to dance, let the fun begin!

Jars on shelves chuckle in glee,
Reciting the gossip of old cups of tea.
Some swear they've seen shadows flee,
While the ceiling fan twirls in jubilee.

Tales of Spirits Unbound

A friendly ghost tells jokes at dawn,
As curtains swish in a dreamy yawn.
Her poltergeist pals all feel withdrawn,
But they crack up when the vacuum's drawn.

In the attic, old toys have a ball,
Singing a chorus to the dust's soft fall.
With laughter so loud it could wake the hall,
Even the spiders join in for the call.

The wall clock grins as it ticks away,
Counting all the nonsense at play.
Even the stove seems to sizzle in sway,
To the punchlines of spirits that won't decay.

Goblins trade tales of old mishaps,
While shadows stick out their tiny caps.
In a room full of giggles and gentle taps,
Echoes of joy fill in the gaps.

The Pulse of Abandoned Lives

An old chair creaks with a ghostly cheer,
As wallpaper whispers, come lend an ear.
Each scrape on the floor, a laugh sincere,
   Echoing moments from yesteryear.

Beneath the floorboards, secrets reside,
Of mischief and mayhem, where phantoms abide.
Flickering lights offer a playful guide,
As they poke at the past, nothing to hide.

The kitchen's a hub for spirits on break,
While teapots giggle at the cookies they bake.
In this scrappy abode, no serious stake,
Just tales of the silly and none of the fake.

Silly shadows dance on the wall,
Filling the silence with their merry brawl.
From dusk till dawn, they're having a ball,
A pulse of laughter that echoes through all.

Melodies in the Fading Light

In dusk's embraces, tunes softly play,
As whispers of joy swirl and sway.
The rocking chair croons at the end of the day,
Claiming the dusk in a comical way.

Mistress of laughter, the lamp flickers bright,
Casting shadows that skip out of sight.
As the furniture joins in the light-hearted fight,
They conjure up giggles to fill the night.

The echoes of snickers ride on the breeze,
With every creak, they do as they please.
Even the windows laugh with ease,
As the walls sway serenely like dancing trees.

With smiles and tales that refuse to fade,
The night becomes a magical parade.
In a world where the serious is played,
The beauty of jest in silence is laid.

Shadows Dancing with Memory

In the hallway, shadows play,
Whispering secrets, come what may.
They trip on laughter, bump on walls,
Dancing together as the night calls.

A sock from nowhere starts to hum,
Tickled by echoes, what's to come?
The ghost of a cat leaps with joy,
As poltergeists toss a paper toy.

Knocking boots with a wobbly chair,
Winking memories float in the air.
A riddle of time wrapped in glee,
Each chuckle a note in the symphony.

In corners where old stories lie,
They spin around like a pie in the sky.
With every crack, a new joke unfolds,
As shadows laugh, the future beholds.

Resonance of the Unseen

Beneath the floorboards, a banter brews,
With every creak, its comedy cues.
Invisible friends, a giggling squad,
They prank the chairs, and all seem awed.

A whisper floats past the dusty clock,
Tickling the echoes like an old sock.
They chuckle at time, a silly parade,
Each tick of the hand a punchline made.

From walls that bop and windows that sigh,
Came a chorus of laughter, oh my, oh my!
The unseen crowd makes the night bright,
With jesters at play in the ghostly light.

As the curtain of silence starts to fold,
The humor of ages is softly told.
With every beat, a ticklish cheer,
A loving embrace, to draw you near.

The Echo of Heartbeats

In the stillness, beats do collide,
Each thump like a dance, nowhere to hide.
Living echoes bounce from walls so bold,
Whispers of love, a warmth to behold.

A flat-footed ghost tries to groove,
With jazzy steps, it's time to move.
It trips in the rhythm, makes quite the sound,
As heartbeats chuckle, joy abounds.

Laughter rolls in with the midnight air,
No need for silence, no time to spare.
Each heartbeat is a tickle, a pulse of glee,
As spirits sway with the giddy spree.

Moments may fade, yet the giggles remain,
Echoes of laughter, a sweet refrain.
In the dance of the night, we're never apart,
Beats echo on; they warm the heart.

Draped in the Silence of Time

Under drapes of stories untold,
Silence wanders, a jester bold.
Dusted memories twirl and spin,
Tickling the twilight, let's begin.

The clock strikes loud, but joy takes flight,
With every chime, it's a comical sight.
Time throws a prank, makes everyone stare,
As echoes bubble up in the cold night air.

A ghost in the attic tries to chat,
Befriending the shadows, where laughter's at.
With whispers of mischief, the windows swell,
As they hold on tight to the tales they tell.

In this realm, where time stands still,
Every pause is filled with a playful thrill.
So drape yourself in giggles divine,
And dance in the silence; it's all just fine.

Remnants of Lurd: The Forgotten

Once in a room where shadows cling,
Lost socks danced to the ghostly ring.
Chairs whispered secrets of long-lost pies,
And dust bunnies wiggled with gleeful sighs.

A cat in a corner, a king in disguise,
Plotting with mice for a wild surprise.
Creaky floors echo the laughter of years,
While the spoon on the shelf wipes away all the tears.

In the pantry, a pickle jar's charm,
Spilling tales of jam without any harm.
Faded recipes flutter on walls,
As cupcakes giggle in pastry-filled halls.

So gather your ghosts, and come take a trip,
To find joy in laughter, and a forgotten flip.
In a world where the echoes are never quite wrong,
You'll find that the funny is where we belong.

Hallowed Halls of Longing

In halls where the echoes happen to roam,
A dog with a bone claims it as home.
The windows are chatterboxes talking too loud,
While the broom takes a bow, feeling so proud.

Old paintings chuckle, their eyes are in jest,
As they argue who wore the most ridiculous dress.
Spiders spin tales in a web of delight,
On a chandelier swinging in flickering light.

In corners, forgotten, the jellies convene,
To whisper sweet secrets of living unseen.
A squirrel with a hat gives a nod to the crowd,
As the clock strikes a tune that's absurdly loud.

So waltz through these walls with a grin and a wink,
Where echoes are silly, don't stop now to think.
For longing is laughter, a party in disguise,
In the halls of the past where humor still flies.

Time's Breath on the Walls

Time tiptoes lightly, with a grin on its face,
As the tick-tock dances in a curious race.
The wallpaper chuckles, adorned with strange views,
While vintage clocks argue about time-worn news.

Socks on the line, telling tales in the wind,
While the refrigerator hums 'till the daylight is thinned.
Old cobwebs giggle, in velvet-clad nights,
As lanterns flicker like whimsical lights.

A window with secrets spills stories to all,
Of shoes left behind and a forgotten ball.
Time's breath can echo, amusingly free,
In a house full of memories, joyful as can be.

So pause for a moment, hear laughter commence,
In the whispers of hours, the rhythm's intense.
For time wears a mask that's both silly and wise,
In the dance of the walls, the past playfully sighs.

The Residue of Living

In the kitchen, a pot hums a cheery tune,
While forks and knives plan a fork-lifting swoon.
Jars of jelly laugh as they wobble about,
While the cupboard doors gossip, never in doubt.

The scratches on tables tell hilarious tales,
Of feasts that were messy and wild jumpy fails.
With cups clattering sounds, they can't help but cheer,
As the kettle whistles, it's a laugh-a-thon here!

In the garden, the weeds share their comedy show,
As carrots roll in, claiming victory aglow.
Rabbits parade in a whimsical dance,
While worms wiggle their way without any chance.

So savor the silliness, relish the glee,
In a life where the echoes delightfully flee.
The residue of living is laughter unkempt,
In a world where the unusual is truly exempt.

Tides of Old Memories

In corners where laughter used to play,
Ghosts of past joy still dance and sway.
The toaster sings songs of burnt delight,
As socks vanish in the laundry's height.

A chair creaks tales of visitors' schemes,
Whispering secrets of half-forgotten dreams.
The fridge hums the tune of a midnight snack,
While dust bunnies plot their next sneaky attack.

Outside, the wind chuckles with glee,
Playing tag with the old oak tree.
The curtains giggle as they swish and sway,
Holding memories of every silly play.

So join the fun, don't shy away,
In this playful realm where shadows stay.
Laughter echoes from room to room,
Embracing the silliness like sweet perfume.

The Watcher Beneath the Eaves

Up in the rafters, a chair keeps watch,
With a spunky attitude and a quirky notch.
It spies on the mischief that dances below,
As cat-and-dog rivalries put on a show.

The old vacuum grumbles, a reluctant beast,
A monster of dust, but never a feast.
While the broom stands proud, a knight of the night,
Chasing away shadows with bristles held tight.

Chandeliers twinkle, winking with flair,
As dust motes perform in the dimmed air.
The clock ticks loudly, but don't take its hints,
It's just trying to keep up with the quirky prints.

Under the eaves, stories pirouette,
Of laughter and mishaps, how could we forget?
With every creak and echo, we chase some fun,
In a world where the serious never can run.

Hushed Tales of the Still Moments

In the silence, there's giggling trapped in the walls,
   Echoes of pranks and the sound of soft falls.
A spoon playing tag with a mischievous fork,
   In a dance of delight by the old oak's cork.

The clock rolls its eyes at the time that's passed,
While echoes of whispers come whimsically fast.
   The rug gives a chuckle, just under the toes,
   As we step on the memories that tickle and pose.

   Pictures hang loose, with drama to spare,
   Sporting old tales with an amusing flair.
The wallpaper bubbles, it's itching to share,
   Jokes from the past that float in the air.

So hush now, dear friend, lend an ear and you'll see,
   The still moments hum with mischievous glee.
Let laughter resound from the stories that grow,
   In corners of silence where popcorn clouds blow.

Flickers of Memory in the Corners

In corners so snug where shadows spin,
Flickers of laughter invite us to grin.
A catine experiment with cheese and some toast,
Living in excitement, to say the least, the most!

The closet's a stage for a sock puppet show,
Where mismatched socks steal the spotlight's glow.
With each playful flicker, spirits take flight,
Giggling and tumbling through the night.

Dust motes are actors in this silent play,
Reenacting the moments that slipped away.
While a broom holds auditions for roles to portray,
In the theater of memory where giggles convey.

So come and uncover these flickering scenes,
In the nooks of nostalgia where fun intervenes.
As echoes of laughter become the main cast,
In a heartwarming production, forever to last.

Flickering Flames of Lost Voices

In the corner, shadows dance,
A ghostly wiggle, what a chance!
They toss and turn, they trip and slide,
With every flicker, they can't hide.

Laughter echoes, what a scene,
A candle fights with shades of green.
The whispers tease, they pull my hair,
As if to say, 'Come join our scare!'

A poltergeist drops a dish,
"I swear it wasn't me!" comes the wish.
The food goes flying, spirits sing,
A kitchen battle, oh the fling!

So gather 'round for spectral feasts,
With toasted bread and joking beasts.
For in this realm where shadows play,
We'll laugh and dine, come what may!

Reflections in the Shattered Glass

Fragments glimmer, what a sight,
Each shard reflects a ghostly flight.
With silly faces, they appear,
Promising joy, not a single fear.

A bowl of ghouls, who's in the mix?
A game of charades, count the tricks!
They mime my moves, but oh so wrong,
I laugh until it turns to song.

In shattered glass, a truth unfolds,
A linear tale that never molds.
So raise your cup, let's toast this night,
To silly spirits full of light!

Watch as they play in gleeful thrills,
With every laugh, they pay the bills.
At midnight's toll, we'll dance and cheer,
For all these souls bring good-hearted cheer!

Specters at the Window's Edge

At window's edge, they wag their thumbs,
    Making faces, oh the fun!
With glares and grins, they tease the night,
    Playing games in pale moonlight.

"Knock, knock, who's there?" echoes near,
    A ghostly voice that brings good cheer.
The curtains sway; they jump and jive,
    Trying hard just to stay alive!

A spook in shades, with a silly hat,
    Wobbly feet like a kitten's pat.
They tumble down, oh what a sight,
These specters love a comical fright!

So let's all laugh, what a mad crew,
    With every trick, they'll dazzle you.
In windy howls, they pirouette,
    And tell a jest you won't forget!

Secrets wrapped in Midnight Shadows

The midnight clock chimes secrets low,
Wrapped in whispers, tales will flow.
With every tick, a giggle slips,
From shadowed corners, teasing lips.

A riddle danced beneath the bed,
"Where's the ghost?" I laughed instead.
In papers stacked and socks askew,
Those shadows know the tales we brew.

They play their tricks with silly shoes,
And hide in places we might lose.
Under the rug, a mystery clings,
A jester's cap with colorful strings.

So tuck your fears beneath your sheets,
For laughter's here, one of our treats.
In darkened rooms, joy sneaks about,
With midnight secrets, twist and shout!

When Walls Remember

Whispers tickle in the air,
Walls giggle with their flair.
Ghosts play tag from door to door,
Just imagine, who's keeping score?

Laughter echoes, bumps and squeaks,
Nooks and crannies share their tweaks.
Every creak a jolly jest,
In this home, ghosts love to rest.

Pictures grin, they wink and sway,
At this haunted cabaret.
Even shadows join the fun,
At dusk, they chase, till day is done.

Through the hall, they spin and twirl,
Specters giggle, give a whirl.
In the confusion, minds unwind,
A comedic tale, uniquely blind.

Resonance of Longing Hearts

In the attic, secrets sigh,
Phantom lovers look and cry.
Hand in hand, through time they stroll,
Searching for a way to console.

They trip on shoes left in the dark,
One stumbles into a spark.
"What's the rush?" a voice resounds,
"We've got time, and love abounds!"

With blushes bright, they dance with glee,
Chasing echoes, wild and free.
Though their footsteps might be faint,
Every beat makes silence quaint.

Through the rooms, they jumble their words,
Lovebirds chatting, joy absurd.
All around, their laughter roams,
In this space, they find their homes.

Spectral Dance Through the Halls

Twinkle lights like friendly eyes,
Bump along, beneath the skies.
Ghoulish giggles fill the air,
Join the dance, if you dare!

Walls are simply buzzing tunes,
As chandelier sways and swoons.
Caught in a merry ghostly trance,
Who knew they'd love to dance?

Floors may creak like laughter shared,
Watching couch potatoes stared.
In every corner, shadows twine,
Doing the ghostly grapevine.

With a chuckle and a leap,
Specters embrace the night, so deep.
Echoes linger, spirits prance,
In an orbit of flirty trance.

Faded Footsteps on Moonlit Stairs

Up the stairway, echoes creep,
Faded footsteps, can't make them leap.
Tippy-toeing, they tease the night,
With each step, they spark delight.

A waltz begins on cracked old wood,
As they move, it feels so good.
One stumbles, giggles fill the space,
Another says, "let's pick up pace!"

Sneaking shadows, hugging tight,
Causing giggles with every fright.
In the chaos, laughter swells,
Haunted stories weave their spells.

As the moon dips, the steps grow bold,
Whispers turn into stories told.
Here in shadows, spirits prance,
In the glow, they steal their chance.

The Ballad of Weathered Steps

Once I tripped on a crack in the floor,
My cat laughed aloud then ran for the door.
The stairs creaked complaints as I danced down,
Echoes of giggles all over the town.

A rug named old Wilma would quietly sigh,
As I threw my shoes and let out a cry.
The walls whispered secrets to each playful crack,
And the floorboards would jump at the sound of a snack.

In corners where dust bunnies liked to play,
They'd throw wild parties, oh what a day!
With forks in the fridge and spoons on the wall,
The echoes shouted out, "Come one, come all!"

And when I return with a big slice of cake,
Even the fridge hums in a comical shake.
The house holds a laugh in every room,
With memories dancing like a sweet little tune.

Voices of Yesterday's Air

The curtains flung wide, with a dramatic flair,
Whispers and chuckles float up in the air.
Chairs tell old stories, with crackles and squeaks,
While shadows strike poses, as each memory peeks.

The fridge hums a tune that's oddly off-key,
While socks argue playfully, "That's my spot, see!"
The clock on the wall ticks a hilarious beat,
Worn out from jokes that get stuck on repeat.

Old photos all giggle trapped in their frames,
As they share old tales, they play silly games.
With windows wide open, the laughter sails through,
As ghosts in petticoats join in for the brew.

In breezes that tickle, hear stories unfold,
Of friends and of laughter, both timid and bold.
The air carries echoes of joy so sincere,
In rooms filled with memories that tickle the ear.

The Ember of Remembered Smiles

In a room where the past likes to gather and chat,
A pumpkin once sat, wearing my old hat.
It chuckled and blinked with an orange delight,
While shadows jumped jiving until close to night.

The flames in the hearth did the cha-cha and twirl,
As stories of mischief started to unfurl.
They dance with a spirit, all warm and so bright,
Bringing forth echoes of pure delight.

A blanket named Ziggy spins yarns with flair,
Telling jokes to the cushions that wiggle and glare.
The laughter in corners catches dust in its wake,
A playful reminder of all that we make.

And nestled in warmth, with a soft, gentle grace,
The ember sparks smiles that no one can replace.
With quirky reflections, bright laughter will climb,
In the glow of the hearth, old memories chime.

Haunting Melodies of the Past

The piano once played a note far too high,
Causing all chairs to spin round and to fly.
Keyboards giggled and flung off their seats,
As melodies bounced like mischievous fleets.

With ghosts in the hallway practicing tunes,
The chandeliers jingled like playful raccoons.
While the windows stood rattling, pretending to freeze,
The curtains would dance with the slightest of breeze.

A whimsy of echoes, both odd and quite bright,
Gathers the strangers who laugh through the night.
The teacups would clink in an echoing cheer,
As haunting melodies drew in each dear.

And as morning light breaks on joiners who smile,
The house will keep giggling and rest for a while.
With its heart made of joy in every thin wall,
The past remains present, together for all.

Unheard Servants of Time

Tick-tock, the clock goes round,
But no one hears a sound.
Ghosts of chores from days long past,
Mumble as they shuffle fast.

Dust bunnies in a midnight race,
They laugh and spin, a silly chase.
With every sweep, they jump and hide,
While socks in corners plot their stride.

Forgotten things under the bed,
Sneaky snacks and shoes instead.
All vie for a laugh or two,
In this home where mischief grew.

So raise a glass to unheard plight,
Of servants toiling through the night.
In this silly, timeless scheme,
We find joy in every dream.

Bonds of Dust and Light

In the corners dust bunnies loom,
Swaying gently, they make room.
Caught in sunbeams, they dance bright,
Creating chaos, pure delight.

The chairs gossip with creaky news,
About the floors and their worn shoes.
Together they spin tales so funny,
Of spilled milk and a wistful honey.

Lightbulbs flicker, making a spark,
They giggle in the dark.
Shadows stretch and dance with zest,
A nightly show that never rests.

Bonds of dust and light entwined,
A harmony that's well-defined.
In this realm of chuckles bright,
We find joy in every night.

Chorus of Wistful Shadows

Echoes laugh in the hallway's bend,
Whispers of tales the walls defend.
Shadows bounce in corners tight,
Joking 'bout their silly fright.

They play charades in dimmed glow,
With playful antics on show.
A dance of the light with a twisty sway,
As they mock the night and day.

Every flicker brings a grin,
Of timeless tales made of skin.
Wistful chaos does ensue,
When shadows find partners in blue.

Join the waltz, oh brave of heart,
For in the dark, the fun won't part.
A chorus sung in silent tune,
In this evening's merry boon.

Creaks of Time's Embrace

Under the stairs, whispers creep,
Time's embrace brings secrets deep.
The wooden planks squeak with glee,
Sharing jokes, just you and me.

A door that clicks, a window sighs,
Painting tales of disguise.
As mice with tiny twinkling feet,
Join in to share their funny beat.

The walls, they jiggle, dance along,
To a rhythm, sweet and strong.
An orchestra of creaks in tune,
Laughing together in the moon.

So let the echoes fill the air,
We'll chuckle as we stop and stare.
In this quirky, endearing place,
Time's soft laughter leaves a trace.

Lament of Forgotten Echoes

Once there were laughs, now whispers align,
Ghosts play charades, in shadows they twine.
Hiding from dust, their jokes float above,
Tickling the rafters, spread laughter and love.

Old walls creak back, to a forgotten jest,
A skeleton slipped, at a ghostly fest.
Phantoms in bow ties, with a wink and a grin,
Waltzing through memories, they dance and spin.

Echoes of gags, in corners they cling,
Witty remarks that make the walls sing.
A poltergeist groans, "I've got one more pun!"
While shadows all chuckle, "Oh, this is fun!"

Forgotten the sadness, in laughter we bask,
In a spectral retreat, just bring your best mask.
Join this mad party, where levity reigns,
In a realm full of giggles, where no one complains.

Where Silence Breathes

In a room full of echoes, where silence pops,
The walls wear a grin, like mischievous socks.
Forgotten old toys wish for a chance,
To join in the fun, and maybe a dance.

Lurking in corners, the dust bunnies cheer,
While half-empty bottles throw back a beer.
The stillness is crackling, it tickles the air,
Invisible jesters whirl, light as a spare.

Breezy whispers tell tales of old pranks,
As echoes erupt from the shadows with thanks.
A ghost tries a cartwheel, but fumbles the flip,
And laughter erupts with a ghostly old quip.

Oh, the noise of soft silence, it giggles and grins,
Each sigh in the stillness, a tale that begins.
Let's toast to the moments, unseen and discreet,
Where joy visits quietly, and laughter's a treat.

Murmurs of Worn Floors

The floorboards are moaning, a creak and a squeak,
As old wooden planks play hide and seek.
They carry the whispers of footfalls long past,
But now, they're just jiving, their fun unsurpassed.

With the laughter of ages, they chuckle and groan,
Shuffling about in their hardwoody zone.
Each splinter a punchline, each crack a surprise,
As the spirits above exchange giggles and sighs.

With a whoosh and a thump, they start their parade,
The dance of the echoes, a whimsical charade.
While shadows applaud, in this joyous affair,
Spirits join in, and lift off from the air.

The murmurs of floors, a mystery concealed,
Still laugh with abandon, their secrets revealed.
The house breathes with joy, in every creaky space,
Inviting the living to join in the chase.

Spirits in the Attic

Up in the attic, the ruckus is grand,
Where spirits conspire, with games they have planned.
With crates full of memories, they giggle and sneak,
Dropping old nicknames and jokes that they tweak.

A witch's old broom lifts for a spin,
While a ghost in a costume shuffles right in.
They whisper of secrets from days gone by,
Add spice to the attic, as they leap and fly.

With props from the past laid around for delight,
Each cobwebbed corner is part of the night.
They throw little parties in blankets and boxes,
With peculiar guests in mismatched old sockses.

Laughing at echoes that bounce from the wall,
Each spirit a jester, they dance and enthrall.
In the heart of the attic, the laughter ignites,
With spirits so lively, they turn dark into lights.

Fleeting Glimpses of Eternity

In a corner, someone sneezed,
A ghost said, "Bless you, I'm pleased!"
Time flies with a comical wave,
As laughter echoes from beyond the grave.

Chairs twist and turn with glee,
Who knew the past could be such a spree?
A specter waltzes, a dance so spry,
While the cat gives a judgmental eye.

Jokes float like dust in the air,
As the walls shout secrets they dare.
Bubbles of laughter overtake,
Even old shadows can't help but shake.

In the attic, a voice springs forth,
"Did I leave my socks? Oh, what a dearth!"
Eternity's playful, it's true,
Especially for spirits, with much to do!

Echoes that Bind the Past and Present.

In the hallway, whispers fly,
Of a baker who burned a pie.
His spirit grumbles with a frown,
While the oven chuckles, never down.

Yesterday meets today with flair,
A ghostly chef still in his chair.
His apron's stained with tales of old,
As he shares recipes, quite uncontrolled.

Pictures laugh, their eyes aglow,
As relatives argue 'bout the dough.
"My cake was better!" one will boast,
While an old spoon rolls, it's quite a host!

The clock ticks funny, on the wall,
Maintaining time for the spectral ball.
With joy, we remember their way,
Past and present jiving in sway.

Whispers Beneath the Eaves

Beneath the eaves, a mouse once squeaked,
A spirit laughed, "Your future's bleak!"
Yet right after, they shared a snack,
Crumbs of laughter, what a knack!

Footsteps echo, soft as a dream,
Dancing shadows start to beam.
"Did you hear that?" a child will cry,
But it's just the broom, giving a sigh.

The old piano plays a note,
As a specter's voice sings, quite remote.
"Play me something funny, my dear,
Life's too short, let's shift the gear!"

In quiet corners, the echoes lay,
With playful spirits, they dance and sway.
A chuckle here, a giggle too,
In this laughter-filled haunt, where shadows brew.

Shadows in the Hallway

In the hallway, shadows prance,
Trying hard to learn to dance.
One trips over a phantom shoe,
And giggles echo right on cue.

"They say I'm haunted," whispered a chair,
"But it's a riot, beyond compare!"
Voices squeak, like old, creaky springs,
As laughter flutters on ghostly wings.

Lights flicker, casting a grin,
A shadow peeks from a cupboard within.
"Let's play hide-and-seek again tonight,
I'll be the ghost, you won't see my light!"

In corners dim, chuckles bloom,
With every echo, dispelling the gloom.
Letting jest and joy redefine,
These shadows know how to shine.

Gaze upon the Unforgotten

In shadows where the old ghosts play,
They chuckle and dance, not far away.
While dusty books spill secrets bold,
They giggle at tales that should never be told.

An old cat purrs with a cheeky grin,
Who knew that spirits could be such a spin?
With every creak and every laugh,
They weave the past in a silly half.

A wig on a mannequin, a lopsided hat,
Those echoes of yore are quite the format.
As shivers mix with bursts of glee,
Ghostly pranks on you and me.

So gather round, give a light cheer,
For wacky whispers fill the air here.
In laughter we find the tales anew,
Where memories snag a giggle or two.

Whispers of the Cold Stone

From beneath the gravel, whispers creep,
Stone-hearted tales that never sleep.
A ruckus of laughter from the stones,
They giggle and tease, in hushed tones.

A ghost with a flick of a playful wand,
Sings lullabies of a far-off pond.
Cracking jokes in a cackle so loud,
These stony souls form a chuckling crowd.

Mischief swirls like dust in the air,
As poltergeists pull pranks full of flair.
Rumbling laughter echoes 'round the walls,
Turning hollow halls into slapstick balls.

So sit on the stone, don't be afraid,
Those playful spirits have fine parades.
With every whisper of the cold stone,
Lies a humorous spark in the unknown.

Songs of the Untold Histories

In the attic where the lost tunes float,
Are liars, jesters, and a silly goat.
They sing of things long buried and pale,
Mixing laughter like a quirky tale.

A chorus of hiccups from a dusty past,
Echoing secrets, now at last.
Quips about kings with unruly hair,
And queens in gowns too wide to wear.

Tickling the air with an ancient rhyme,
While chimneys sway in flow of time.
They prank the clocks and wink at the moon,
Creating mischief in a playful tune.

So sway to the songs of histories untold,
Where humor and mischief spark up the bold.
With every laugh, these old tales unfold,
In the echoes of laughter that never grow old.

Spirits Stirring in the Gloaming

In twilight's hush, a giggle breaks,
As spirits dance and the candle quakes.
They rustle leaves with a wink and a smile,
Plotting their pranks with mischievous style.

Owls hoot softly, in on the joke,
While the old tree creaks with a humorous poke.
Spinning tales of a lost sock or shoe,
In twilight's grip where giggles ensue.

With every shadow, a spirit will play,
Sneaking up close, then dancing away.
Chasing moonbeams with bursts of delight,
In the gloaming they twirl, a whimsical sight.

So as night draws near, raise a glass or two,
To spirits who tease and always renew.
For in laughter lies a magic so deep,
Where joy echoes softly, and never sleeps.

www.ingramcontent.com/pod-product-compliance
Lightning Source LLC
Chambersburg PA
CBHW060146230426
43661CB00003B/583